HYSTERICAL HOCKEY
JOKES AND PUNS

Text by Benjamin Bird

T0403227

STONE ARCH BOOKS
a capstone imprint

Published by Stone Arch Books,
an imprint of Capstone.
1710 Roe Crest Drive
North Mankato, Minnesota 56003
capstonepub.com

Library of Congress Cataloging-in-Publication Data is
available on the Library of Congress website.

ISBN: 9798875220920 (hardcover)
ISBN: 9798875220883 (paperback)
ISBN: 9798875220890 (ebook PDF)

Summary: A collection of hockey-themed jokes and puns
perfect for fans of the sport.

Designer: Dina Her

Design Elements: Nana Chen, Shutterstock: Vector FX

Printed and bound in China. 006276

TABLE OF CONTENTS

SECTION 1: TEAM TICKLERS

Where do the Devils players get their uniforms?

New Jersey, of course!

What do the Tampa Bay Lightning players wear under their uniforms?

Thunderwear!

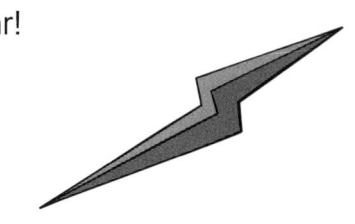

Why did the Oilers bring a fire extinguisher to their game against Calgary?

To stop the Flames.

Why did the Dallas Stars bring musical instruments to St. Louis?

To play the Blues.

Why does the Dallas hockey team win so many games?

Because they're all Stars.

Why do the Minnesota Wild players drink from bowls?

Because they don't have any Cups.

Why can't the Sharks ever win?

They're always afraid of the net!

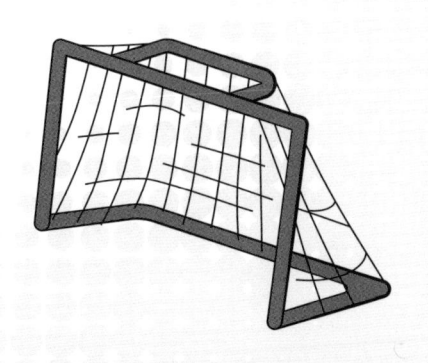

Why do the Los Angeles Kings always wear crowns?

Because they rule the ice.

Why do the Las Vegas Golden Knights shine so bright?

Because they always wear their armor.

What happens when the Lightning win a game?

The fans are shocked.

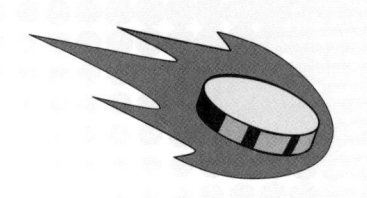

What penalty are the Buffalo Sabres players often called for?

Slashing!

What do Coyotes and Panthers have in common?

Neither of them can skate.

Why don't Columbus fans ever get cold at the arena?

Because of their Blue Jackets.

Why did the New York fans all go home sick?

They had Islanders fever.

What do you call a Boston Bruins player with no teeth?

A gummy bear.

Why did the Mighty Ducks player get ejected from the game?

Fowl play.

Why did the Toronto kid climb up a tree with a hockey stick?

Because they wanted to join the Maple Leafs.

What's King Charles's favorite hockey team?

The Los Angeles Kings.

How do the Seattle Kraken travel from game to game?

An octo-bus.

Why do the Boston Bruins disappear once the hockey season starts?

Because bears hibernate during the winter.

Why don't the Ducks play teams from northern states?

They fly south in the winter.

What is a St. Louis hockey player's favorite color?

Blue, of course!

When should hockey players wear armor?

When they play Knight games.

Where do Wild players get their equipment?

Beast Buy.

What time do Las Vegas hockey players prefer to play?

Knight time.

What did the Buffalo Sabres player tell his son when he left for the game?

"Bison!"

What do you call an Anaheim Duck that gets straight As?

A wisequacker.

How many tickles does it take to make a Seattle Kraken player laugh?

Ten-tickles.

What do you call a Penguin at the North Pole?

Lost!

Why does Dallas only play after dark?

Because Stars only shine at night.

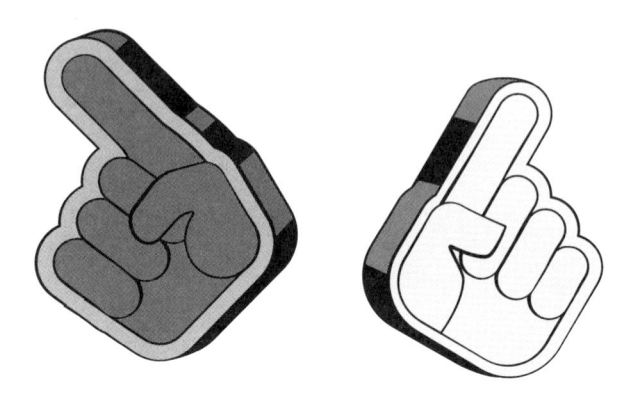

How do the Anaheim Ducks celebrate a win?

With firequackers.

Why do the Penguins always take the bus to away games?

Because they can't fly.

What did the Hurricanes' goalie say to the puck?

"I've got my eye on you!"

Why did the rookie goalie leave the game?

He got cold feet.

What did the hockey goalie say to the puck?

"Catch you later!"

Why was the goalie sitting down and drinking tea?

Because someone put a biscuit in his basket.

What is a ghost's favorite position in hockey?

Ghoulkeeper.

Why do goalies wear masks for Halloween?

Because they always do.

Why did the goalie change his pants?

Because he had five holes in them.

How do hockey goalies catch up on sleep?

They catch some Zs.

What's the best game plan for any hockey player?

A dental plan.

Why did the hockey goalie bring his mitt to the beach?

To catch some rays.

How was the goalie able to retire early?

He spent all his time saving.

Why was the hockey team's goalie always getting picked on?

He was a big target.

Where does a hockey goalie keep their glove while driving?

In the glove compartment.

What did the hockey puck say to the goalie?

"I'm totally lost—can you help me find my net?"

Why don't hockey goalies iron their uniforms?

They like to defend the crease.

Why did the coach get frustrated when he checked his email?

He had too many forwards.

Why was Cinderella such a lousy hockey player?

Because her coach was a pumpkin.

Why did the hockey coach draft a mummy?

Because he had a nice wraparound.

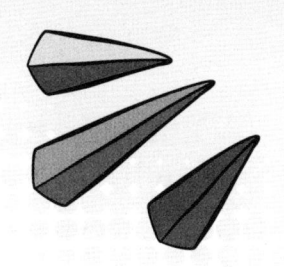

Why was the hockey coach so full after the game?

His team had too many turnovers.

Why did the coach hire a T. rex to play for him?

His team needed more shorthanded goals.

Why did the coach tell his goalie to bring a tree to the arena?

Because he'd be riding the pine all game.

What did the hockey coach do after he retired?

He became a dentist!

What is a hockey coach's favorite color?

Yeller!

Why did the hockey coach ask a tiny ghost to join the hockey team?

They needed a little team spirit.

SLAPSTICK COMEDY

Why did the hockey player bring a camera to the game?

To capture all the shots on goal.

Why are hockey rinks always rounded?

Because if they were ninety degrees, then the ice would melt.

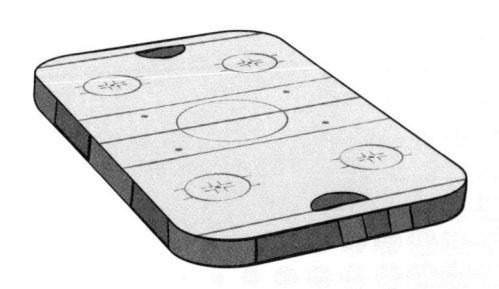

Why did the hockey team call an exterminator?

The stadium was filled with rink rats!

Why are ice hockey players never nervous?

Because they're all super chill.

Why don't dogs play hockey?

They always get penalized for ruffing.

Why was the hockey player such a bad actor?

They were always changing their lines.

What do hockey players say on Halloween?

"Hat trick or treat!"

How many hockey players can jump higher than a crossbar?

All of them—a crossbar can't jump.

Why did the hockey puck quit the game?

It was tired of being slapped around.

Why did the hockey player bring a ladder to the game?

To work on his high-sticking.

Why did the hockey player visit the library?

To check out some new plays.

PENALTY PUNS

Why did the superheroes meet at the playground?

For a power play.

Why was there a barber in the penalty box?

He got two minutes for clipping.

Why did the hockey player smell brand new?

They just came out of the box.

How can you tell that hockey referees are happy?

They whistle while they work.

Why did the referee get a new phone?

Because they had been missing calls all season.

What is black and white and red all over?

An embarrassed referee.

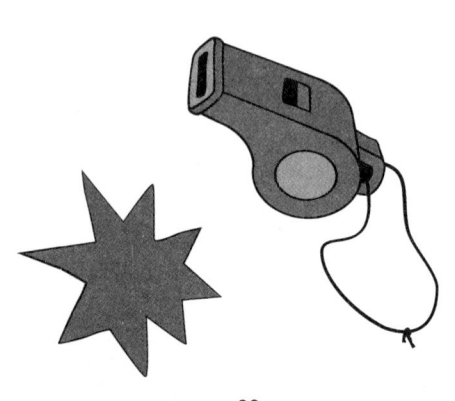

Why did the hockey players get arrested during a power play?

For penalty killing.

Why didn't the hockey player bring his credit cards to the game?

He didn't want to be penalized for charging.

Did you hear about the referee that got fired from the NHL?

Supposedly they were a whistleblower.

EQUIPMENT FUNNIES

What do you call a Penguin helmet?

An ice cap.

Which hockey player has the biggest skates?

The one with the biggest feet.

Why do hockey players have numbers on their jerseys?

To remember how many teeth they've lost.

What kind of hockey skates wear out quickly?

Cheapskates!

Why was the hockey player chewing on the puck?

He heard it was a biscuit.

Why did the hockey player wear a sweater to the game?

To warm up his shots.

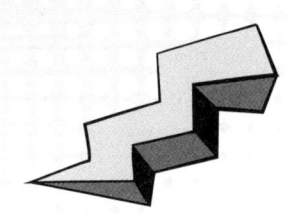

Why did the hockey player bring extra socks?

In case he got cold feet.

Why did the hockey player bring a flashlight?

To find the puck in the dark.

If a hockey player gets athlete's foot, what does an astronaut get?

Missile toe.

ONE-LINER LAUGHS

What kind of tea do hockey players drink?

Penal-tea.

Why did the hockey player call in sick?

They had a bad case of chicken pucks.

Why do hockey players make great friends?

Because they always stick together.

Why don't pigs play hockey?

They always hog the puck.

What's the hardest part about hockey?

The ice.

What's the difference between a hockey game and a wrestling match?

In a hockey game, the fights are real.

Why don't hockey players like to play hide-and-seek?

Because good defense is hard to find!

What's a hockey player's favorite board game?

Check-ers!

What's a hockey fan's favorite drink?

Root beer.

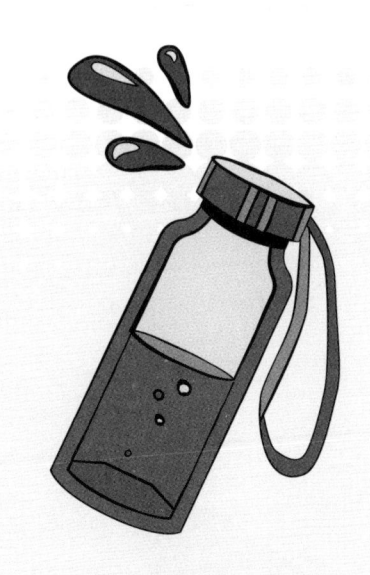

How do hockey players kiss?

They puck-er up.

What's a hockey player's favorite vegetable?

Ice-berg lettuce.

Why do hockey players love donuts?

They can't resist the icing.

What's a hockey player's favorite weather?

Freezing rain.

What's a hockey player's second favorite game?

Freeze tag.

What do you call a smart hockey player?

A sharpshooter.

Why did the hockey player join the army?

To be on the front line.

What's a hockey player's favorite vacation spot?

Iceland.

What has twelve feet and sticks on ice?

A hockey team.

What is the hardest foot to buy a hockey skate for?

A square foot.

How did a dog make the all-star team?

He was the league's best stickhandler.

Why did the fan bring extra money to the game?

In case she spotted a yard sale.

Why did the hockey player fail English class?

Every sentence had three periods.

What is harder to catch the faster you skate?

Your breath!

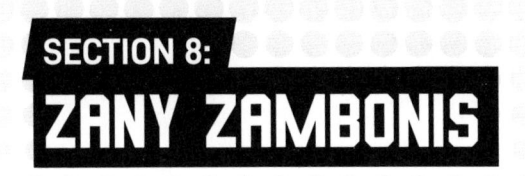

SECTION 8:
ZANY ZAMBONIS

Why did the detective drive a Zamboni?

To clear up the cold cases.

What did the Zamboni say to the hockey player?

"Ice to meet you."

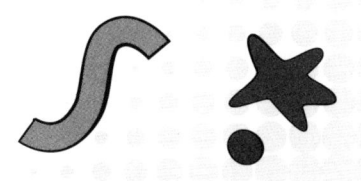

What did the zombie ride at the hockey rink?

The Zombie-oni.

Why didn't the police search for the missing Zamboni driver?

Because he always resurfaces.

What did the cowboy ride to the hockey game?

A Zam-pony.

Why did the pasta chef go to the hockey game?

To ride the Zam-roni.

What did the skeleton drive to the hockey game?

The Zam-bony.

SECTION 9:
ICEBREAKERS

Why was the hockey team delayed at the airport?

All the players were getting checked.

What does a hockey player do on vacation?

They take a breakaway.

What happened to the hockey player who demanded more money?

He was given a check.

What do you call a hockey player with a great sense of humor?

A slapstick comedian.

What is it called when a T. rex gets a goal?

A dino-score.

Why was the ghost always left out in a hockey game?

Because he had no *body* to play with.

What was the hockey player's favorite snack?

Goal-fish crackers.

What do you call a hockey player who can't score?

A defenseman.

Why don't hockey players ever run for office?

Because they're better at skating.

Why did the hockey player bring string to the game?

So they could tie the score.

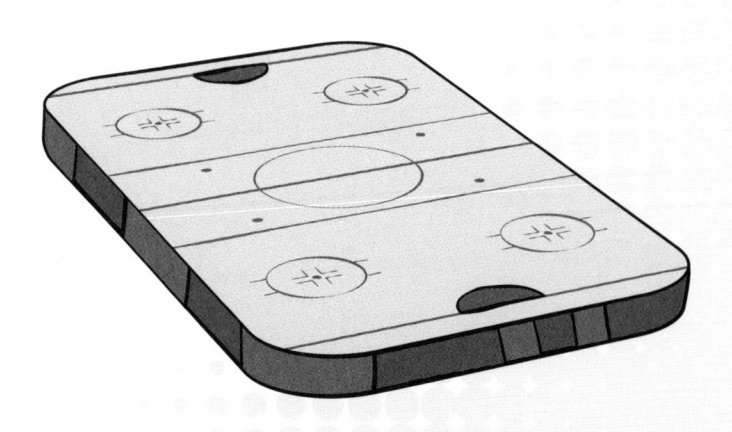

Why did the hockey player bring an iron to the rink?

To avoid a crease violation.

Why don't hockey players wear eyeglasses?

It's a contact sport.

Why do hockey players never make friends?

They don't want to break the ice.

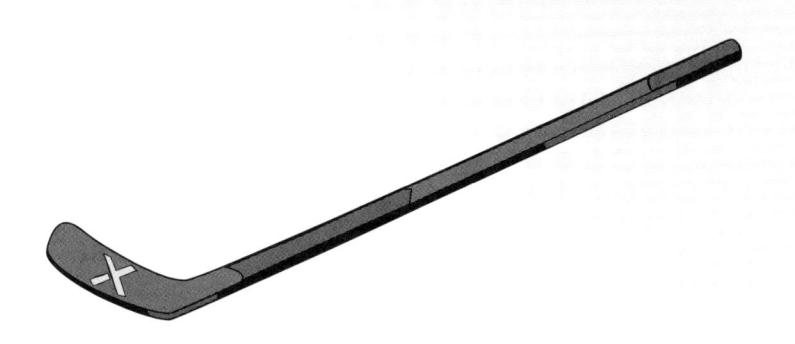

What are successful forwards always trying to do?

Reach goals.

Why do people say that carpenters cannot play hockey?

They always get nailed to the boards.

What is another word for a hockey fan?

A Canadian.

Why do cowboys like hockey so much?

Because of all the shoot-outs.

Where do hockey players get all their money?

The tooth fairy.

Why did the hockey player bring a match to the game?

To light the lamp.

What bug is best at hockey?

A stick insect.

What's the hockey player's favorite fairy tale?

Goal-dilocks and the Three Bears.

Why did the hockey player go to jail?

Because he shot the puck.

Why are the Swiss bad hockey players?

They never leave the neutral zone.

Why didn't the dog want to play hockey?

It was a boxer.

Why can't anyone possibly play hockey in a jungle?

There are just too many cheetahs.

Did you hear the joke about the high stick?

Forget it—it's way over your head.

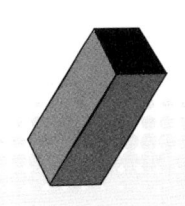

What's the difference between a puck hog and time?

Time passes.

Why did the hockey player become a magician?

They loved hat tricks.

What do you get when you cross the Penguin's all-star player with a cat?

Mario Lem-meow.

Why couldn't Wayne Gretzky listen to music?

He broke all the records.

What's a hockey player's favorite type of sandwich?

Ice-burgers.

What do hockey players eat before a game?

Puck-eroni pizza!

What's a hockey player's favorite kind of party?

A goal-together.

What did the hockey player say when he got angry?

"No more Mr. Ice Guy!"

Why did the hockey player bring a pen to the game?

To draw up some winning plays.

What is the difference between a bad hockey team and the Bermuda Triangle?

The Bermuda Triangle has three points.

What's the difference between a bad hockey team and an eagle?

An eagle has got two decent wings.

How are a bad hockey team and the *Titanic* alike?

They both look good until they hit the ice.

Why do hockey rinks melt after the game?

All the fans leave.

What runs around a hockey team but never moves?

The boards.

How are scrambled eggs and bad hockey teams the same?

They've both been beaten!

What's a hockey enforcer's favorite drink?

Punch.

Why don't hairdressers like hockey?

They prefer figure skating.

What's a hockey player's favorite type of metal?

Goooooooooooooold!

What time of year do hockey players get injured the most?

In the fall.

Two silkworms played hockey. Who won?

It was a tie.

Why do ice hockey players not like field hockey?

Because it's not as cool.

Why are hockey players known for their summer teeth?

Because summer here, summer there.

How many teeth does a hockey player have?

Don't you mean tooth?

How are hockey players like goldfish?

You can tap on the glass to get their attention.

Why was the hockey rink wet?

Because people were dribbling on it.

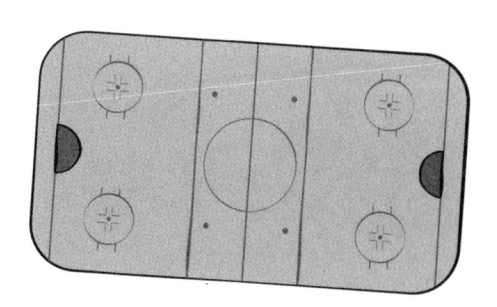

Who played ice hockey before it was cool?

Swimmers.

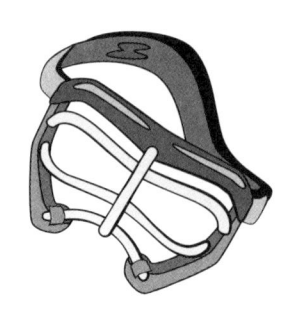

What is the best way to decorate a hockey player's birthday cake?

With lots of icing.

What do you call a hockey rink in summer?

A puddle.

 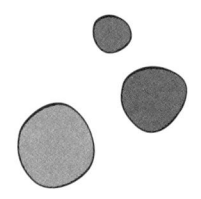

How do hockey players make their beds?

With sheets of ice.

What do hockey players call their kids?

Chill-dren.

TELLING FUNNY JOKES!

1. Know your joke.

Be sure you memorize the whole joke before you tell it. Most of us have heard someone start a joke by saying, "Oh, this is SO funny . . ." But then they can't remember part of it. Or they forget the ending, which is the most important part of the joke—the punch line!

2. Speak up.

Don't mumble your words. And don't speak too fast or too slow. Just speak clearly. You don't have to use a strange voice or accent. (Unless that's part of the joke!)

3. Look at your audience.

Good eye contact with your listeners will grab and hold their attention.

4. Don't overthink things.

You don't need to use silly gestures to tell your joke, unless it helps sell the punch line. You can either sit or stand to tell your jokes. Make yourself comfortable. Remember, telling jokes is basically just talking to people to make them laugh.

5. Don't laugh at your own joke.

Sure, comedians sometimes crack up laughing while they're telling a story. And that can be pretty funny by itself. But normally, it's best not to laugh at your own jokes. If you do, you might lose the timing of your joke or mess it up. Let your audience do the laughing. Your job is to be the funny one.

6. Practice your setup.

The setup is the second most important part of a joke. This includes everything you say before getting to the punch line. Be as clear as you can so when you reach the punch line, it makes sense!

7. Get the punch line right.

The punch line is the most important part of the joke. It's the payoff to the main event. A good joke is best if you pause for a second or two before delivering the punch line. That tiny pause will make your audience pay attention, eager to hear what's coming next.

8. Practice, practice, practice.

Practice your routine until you know it by heart. You can also watch other comedians or a comedy show or film. Listen to other people tell a joke. Pay attention to what makes them funny. You can pick up skills by seeing how others get an audience laughing. With enough practice, you'll soon be a great comedian.

9. It's all about the timing.

Learn to get the timing right for the biggest impact. Waiting for the right time and giving that extra pause before the punch line can really zing an audience. But you should also know when NOT to tell a joke. You probably know when your friends like to hear something funny. But when around unfamiliar people, you need to "read the room" first. Are people having a good time? Or is it a more serious event? A joke is funniest when it's told in the right setting.

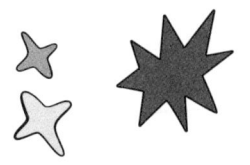

HOCKEY TERMS TO KNOW

breakaway (BREY-kuh-wey)—when a player skates alone toward the opponent's goal with no defenders blocking their path

checking (CHEH-king)—the act of using one's body to knock an opponent against the boards or to the ice to disrupt their play

face-off (FEYS-awf)—the method used to begin play, where two opposing players try to gain control of the puck after it is dropped by an official

hat trick (HAT TRIK)—when a player scores three goals in a single game

offside (AWF-sahyd)—a violation that occurs when an offensive player enters the opponent's zone before the puck

penalty box (PEH-nuhl-tee BOKS)—the area where players serve time for penalties they have committed

power play (POU-ur PLAY)—a situation in which one team has more players on the ice due to one or more opposing players serving a penalty

slashing (slash-ing)—a penalty called when a player swings their stick at an opponent, regardless of whether contact is made

GLOSSARY

exterminator (ek-STER-muh-nay-ter)—a person whose job is to get rid of bugs and pests

forward (FOR-werd)—hockey players who play near the opponent's goal to try to score

goalie (GOH-lee)—the player who tries to stop the puck from going into the net

hibernate (HAHY-ber-neyt)—to spend the winter in a resting state

penalty (PEN-l-tee)—a punishment for breaking the rules in a game

spectator (SPEK-tey-ter)—a person who watches a game or event

turnovers (TUR-noh-verz)—when the puck is taken away by the other team

ABOUT THE AUTHOR

Benjamin Bird is a children's book editor and freelance writer from St. Paul, Minnesota. He has written books about some of today's most popular characters, including Batman, Superman, Wonder Woman, Scooby-Doo, Tom & Jerry, and many more.

READ THEM ALL!

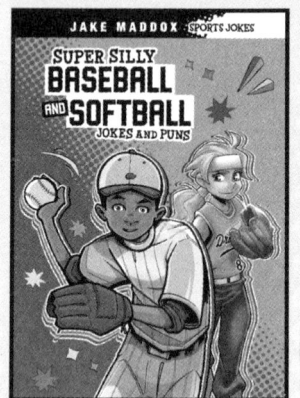